MAX on life
cd-book :: study

Becoming
Money Smart

:: 4 Interactive Bible Studies
for Individuals or Small Groups

MAX LUCADO

THOMAS NELSON PUBLISHERS

CONTENTS

HOW TO USE
THIS STUDY GUIDE

Congratulations! You are making God's Word a priority. These moments of reflection will change you forever. Here are a few suggestions for you to get the most out of your individual study.

1

As you begin each study, pray that God will speak to you through his Word.

2

Read the overview to each study, then listen to the audio segment, taking notes on the worksheet provided.

3

Following the audio segment, respond to the personal Bible study and reflection questions. These questions are designed to take you deeper into God's Word and help you focus on God and on the theme of the study.

4

There are three types of questions used in the study. *Observation* questions focus on the basic facts: who, what, when, where, and how. *Interpretation* questions delve into the meaning of the passage. *Application* questions help you get practical: discovering the implications of the text for growing in Christ. These three keys will help you unlock the treasures of Scripture.

5

Write your answers to the questions in the spaces provided or in a personal journal. Writing brings clarity and deeper understanding of yourself and of God's Word.

6

Keep a Bible dictionary handy. Use it to look up any unfamiliar words, names, or places.

7

Have fun! Studying God's Word can bring tremendous rewards to your life. Allow the Holy Spirit to illuminate your mind to the amazing applications each study can have in your daily life. ■

INTRODUCTION

BECOMING MONEY SMART

In 1900 the average person living in the United States wanted seventy-two different things and considered eighteen of them essential. Today the average person wants five hundred things and considers one hundred of them essential.

Our obsession with stuff carries a hefty price tag. The average American family devotes a full one-fourth of its spendable income to outstanding debts. We spend 110 percent of our disposable income trying to manage debt. And who can keep up? We no longer measure ourselves against the Joneses next door but against the star on the screen or the stud on the magazine cover. Hollywood's diamonds make yours look like a gumball-machine toy. Who can satisfy Madison Avenue? No one can. For that reason Jesus warns, "Be careful and guard against all kinds of greed. Life is not measured by how much one owns" (Luke 12:15).

Greed comes in many forms. Greed for approval. Greed for applause. Greed for status. Greed for the best office, the fastest car, the prettiest date. Greed has many faces, but speaks only one language: the language of more. Epicurus noted, "Nothing is enough for the man to whom enough is too little." And what was that observation from John D. Rockefeller's? He was asked, "How much money does it take to satisfy a man?" He answered, "Just a little more." Wise was the one who wrote, "Whoever loves money will never have enough money; whoever loves wealth will not be satisfied with it. This is also useless" (Eccle. 5:10).

Greed has a growling stomach. Feed it, and you risk more than budget-busting debt. You risk losing purpose. Don't let the itch for things derail you from your God-intended design and your ability to become money smart. ■

As soon as you can, pay your debts.
As long as you can, give the benefit of the doubt.
As much as you can, give thanks.
He's already given us more than we deserve.

MAX LUCADO

LESSON ONE:

RULES
OF THE
KINGDOM

*Even wise people are fools if they let
money change their thinking.*

ECCLESIASTES 7:7

OVERVIEW

God's foremost rule of finance is: We owe nothing. We are managers, not owners. Stewards, not landlords. Maintenance people, not proprietors. Our money is not ours; it is his.

The rich man in Luke 12 gave no thought to that. Please note that Jesus didn't criticize this man's affluence. He criticized his arrogance. The rich man's words testify to his priority.

This rich man was aggressively self-centered. His world was fenced in by himself. He was blind. He didn't see God. He didn't see others. He saw only self.

> *This is what I will do:*
> *I will tear down . . .*
> *I will store . . .*
> *Then I can say to myself, "I have enough good things."*
> Luke 12:18-19

Strange, isn't it, that this rich man had enough sense to acquire wealth but not enough to get ready for eternity? Stranger still, that we make the same mistake. It's not as if God kept the future a secret. One glance at a cemetery should remind us: everyone dies. One visit to a funeral should convince us: we don't take anything with us.

Hearses pull no U-Hauls.

Dead men push no ten-million-dollar wheelbarrows.

If greed costs you your faith or family, the price is too high.

PART 1:
FOLLOW-ALONG NOTES

USE THIS WORKSHEET AS YOU LISTEN TO "BECOMING MONEY SMART, PART 1."

- Luke 5:1-11

- There are over _____ references in the Bible to money management.

- There is a direct relationship with our attitude about money and eternal peace.

RULES OF THE KINGDOM

- God is the _____ and we are the managers.

- God is the _____ and we are the fishermen.

REASONS THAT GOD GIVES US MONEY

1. _____

   1 Timothy 5:8

2. _____

   Romans 13:8

3. _____

   Proverbs 19:17

   Micah 7:18

4. _____

   1 Corinthians 9:7

- Being kind to the poor is like lending to the LORD; he will reward you for what you have done.

  Proverbs 19:17

PART 2:
GOING DEEPER

PERSONAL STUDY AND REFLECTION

- Share your thoughts on the relationship between a person's attitude about money and eternal life.

_____

_____

_____

_____

_____

· Based on the reasons given why God gives us money, how does that affect
  your attitude about the money you earn?

_____

_____

_____

_____

_____

_____

· *The supreme rule when it comes to our possessions: God is the owner, and we
  are the managers.*

· How will you implement changes in your spending habits based on the
  knowledge that God is the owner and we are just the managers?

_____

_____

_____

_____

· **Read Matthew 19:13-24**. Share your thoughts on the good and the bad in
  the life of the rich young ruler.

_____

_____

_____

_____

- As you reflect on the story of Peter, what do you think he was thinking when Jesus asked for the use of the boat?

_____

_____

_____

_____

_____

_____

_____

_____

- *It is wise to let Jesus get into the very place where you work.*

- Have there been times you refused Jesus use of "your boat?" Share what you wish you had done differently in those moments.

_____

_____

_____

_____

_____

_____

_____

_____

_____

· List the financial principles given in the following verses:

Matthew 7:7-11 _____

_____

Matthew 6:19-20 _____

_____

Romans 4:4 _____

_____

Romans 1:25 _____

_____

Romans 8:12 _____

_____

If your riches are yours,
why don't you take them with you
to the other world?

Benjamin Franklin

LESSON TWO:

ATTITUDES TO AVOID

You cannot serve both God and worldly riches.

MATTHEW 6:24

OVERVIEW

Jesus had a definition for greed. He called it the practice of measuring life by possessions in Luke 12:16-21.

Greed equates a person's worth with a person's purse.

1. You got a lot = you are a lot.

2. You got a little = you are little.

The consequences of such a philosophy are predictable. If you are the sum of what you own, then by all means own it all. No price is too high. No payment is too much.

Now, very few would be guilty of blatant greed. Jesus knew that. That's why he cautioned against "all kinds of greed" (Luke 12:15). Greed wears many faces.

When we lived in Rio de Janeiro, Brazil, I went to visit a member of our church. He had been a strong leader in the congregation, but for several Sundays we didn't see or hear from him.

Friends told me he had inherited some money and was building a house. I found him at the construction site. He'd inherited three hundred dollars. With the money, he'd purchased a tiny lot adjacent to a polluted swamp. The plot of land was the size of a garage. On it he was, by hand, constructing a one-room house. He gave me a tour of the project—it took about twenty seconds.

We sat in front and talked. I told him we'd missed him, that the church needed him back. He grew quiet and turned and looked at his house. When he turned again his eyes were moist.

"You're right, Max," he confessed, "I guess I just got greedy."

Greedy? I wanted to say. *You're building a hut in a swamp and you call it greed?* But I didn't say anything because he was right. Greed is relative. Greed is not defined by what something costs; it is measured by what it costs you.

If anything costs you your faith or your family, the price is too high.

PART 1:
FOLLOW-ALONG NOTES

USE THIS WORKSHEET AS YOU LISTEN TO "BECOMING MONEY SMART, PART 2."

ATTITUDES THAT GOD WILL NOT BLESS

1. _____ (Proverbs 11:24)

2. _____ (Proverbs 21:5)

3. _____ (Proverbs 18:13)

4. _____ (Proverbs 20:13)

5. _____ (Proverbs 23:21)

6. _____ (Proverbs 28:19)

The proper attitude towards money: _____

PART 2:
GOING DEEPER

PERSONAL STUDY AND REFLECTION

- Based on the list of attitudes that God does not honor, which give you the
  most difficulty?

_____

_____

_____

_____

_____

_____

· **Read Deuteronomy 10:14-15.** According to the passage, why does greed make no sense?

_____

_____

_____

_____

_____

_____

_____

_____

· *God doesn't bless a stingy heart.*

- How does society affect your ability to keep the right attitude about money?

_____

_____

_____

_____

_____

- But _____ yourselves with the _____ _____

_____ and forget about _____ your _____

self.

Romans 13:14

- **Read Hebrews 13:5-6.** What negative command and positive command do we find in this Scripture? What reason is given to obey the commands? What results from obedience of the commands?

_____

_____

_____

_____

_____

_____

- *Don't make major purchases without giving it time, thought, and prayer.*

- Define in your own words the proper attitude towards money and all other possessions that God will honor.

_____

_____

_____

_____

_____

_____

_____

_____

_____ ■

A thousand regrets do not cancel one debt.

TURKISH PROVERB

LESSON THREE:

DEALING WITH DEBT

Pay everyone, then, what you owe.

ROMANS 13:7

OVERVIEW

Come with me to the most populated prison in the world. The facility has more inmates than bunks. More prisoners than plates. More residents than resources.

Come with me to the world's most oppressive prison. Just ask the inmates; they will tell you. They are overworked and underfed. Their walls are bare and bunks are hard.

No prison is so populated, no prison so oppressive, and what's more, no prison is so permanent. Most inmates never leave. They never escape. They never get released. They serve a life sentence in this overcrowded, underprovisioned facility.

The name of the prison? You'll see it over the entrance. Rainbowed over the gate are four cast-iron letters that spell out its name:

W-A-N-T

The prison of want. You've seen her prisoners. They are "in want." They want something. They want something bigger. Nicer. Faster. Thinner. They want.

They don't want much, mind you. They want just one thing. One new job. One new car. One new house. One new spouse. They don't want much. They want just one.

And when they have "one," they will be happy. And they are right—they will be happy. When they have "one," they will leave the prison. But then it happens. The new-car smell passes. The new job gets old. The neighbors buy a larger television set. The sizzle fizzles, and before you know it, another ex-con breaks parole and returns to jail.

Are you in prison? You are if you feel better when you have more and worse when you have less. You are if joy is one delivery away, one transfer away, one award away, or one makeover away. If your happiness comes from something you deposit, drive, drink, or digest, then face it—you are in prison, the prison of want.

That's the bad news. The good news is, you have a visitor. And your visitor has a message that can get you paroled. Make your way to the receiving room. Take your seat in the chair, and look across the table at the psalmist David. He motions for you to lean forward, "I have a secret to tell you," he whispers, "the secret of satisfaction. "The LORD is my shepherd; I shall not want'" (Ps. 23:1 NKJV).

David has found the pasture where discontent goes to die. It's as if he is saying, "What I have in God is greater than what I don't have in life."

You think you and I could learn to say the same?

Think for just a moment about the things you own. Think about the house you have, the car you drive, the money you've saved. Think about the jewelry you've inherited and the stocks you've traded and the clothes you've purchased. Envision all your stuff, and let me remind you of two biblical truths.

Your stuff isn't yours. Ask any coroner. Ask any funeral-home director. No one takes anything with him. And you know what else abut all that stuff? *It's not you.* Who you are has nothing to do with the clothes you wear or the car you drive. Heaven does not know you as the fellow with the nice suit or the woman with the big house or the kid with the new bike. Heaven knows your heart.

Define yourself by your stuff, and you'll feel good when you have a lot and bad when you don't.

As you deal with financial debt, make sure it wasn't caused by too much "want."

PART 1:
FOLLOW-ALONG NOTES

USE THIS WORKSHEET AS YOU LISTEN TO "BECOMING MONEY SMART, PART 3."

Practical definition of debt:_____

_____

ESTABLISH A PERSONAL LOAN APPLICATION
TO AVOID DEBT

Before buying, ask yourself:

1. Are you robbing God?

Malachi 3:8

Debt reflects a:

_____ heart

Luke 12:15

_____ heart

Proverbs 21:17

_____ heart

Psalm 37:5

2. Are you robbing yourself?   Proverbs 30:25

When you are using credit card debt, you are not _____.

3. Are you robbing your peace?

Proverbs 12:25
Proverbs 22:7

Why did God allow debt?

Deuteronomy 15:1-11

To encourage _____

To acknowledge _____

To protect _____

4. Are you robbing your integrity?

Psalm 37:21
Psalm 37:16

The greatest danger of debt _____.

PART 2:
GOING DEEPER

PERSONAL STUDY AND REFLECTION

· What are the excuses made to justify credit card debt?

_____

_____

_____

_____

_____

_____

_____

• How has credit card debt affected our families and our nation?

_____

_____

_____

_____

_____

_____

_____

_____

_____

• *Debt-ridden nations are made up of debt-ridden families.*

- Explain how debt destroys the ability to have peace.

  _____

  _____

  _____

  _____

- Listen to my _____, and you will be _____; do

  not _____ it.   Proverbs 8:33

- Wisdom begins with _____ for the _____, and

  understanding begins with _____ the _____

  _____.   Proverbs 9:10

- If you live _____, you will live a _____ _____;

  wisdom will add _____ to your _____. Proverbs 9:11

- How does the Old Testament plan for dealing with debt differ from your approach to debt?

_____

_____

_____

_____

_____

_____

_____

- Discuss what you consider the greatest danger of debt.

_____

_____

_____

_____

_____

_____

_____

_____

_____ ■

- Now it is time to put some practical effort into dealing with debt. Take a moment to fill out the following chart. By doing so, you have taken the first step to solving the difficulties with debt.

Debt	Payment Plan	Time Frame
_____	_____	_____
_____	_____	_____
_____	_____	_____
_____	_____	_____
_____	_____	_____
_____	_____	_____

In giving, a man receives more than he gives,
and the more is in proportion to the worth of the thing given.

GEORGE MacDONALD

LESSON FOUR:

THE GIFT OF GIVING

Doing what is right is the way to life,
but there is another way that leads to death.

PROVERBS 12:28

OVERVIEW

How does tithing teach you? Consider the simple act of writing a check for the offering. First you enter the date. Already you are reminded that you are a time-bound creature and every possession you have will rust or burn. Best to give it while you can.

Then you enter the name of the one to whom you are giving the money. If the bank would cash it, you'd write *God.* But they won't so you write the name of the church or group that has earned your trust.

Next comes the amount. Ahhh, the moment of truth. You're more than a person with a checkbook. You're David, placing a stone in the sling. You're Peter, one foot on the boat, one foot on the lake. You're a little boy in a big crowd. A picnic lunch is all the Teacher needs, but it's all you have.

What will you do?

Sling the stone? Take a step? Give the meal?

Careful now, don't move too quickly. You aren't just entering an amount . . . you are making a confession. A confession that God owns it all anyway.

And then the line in the lower left-hand corner on which you write what the check is for. Hard to know what to put. It's for light bills and literature. A little bit of outreach. A little bit of salary.

Better yet, it's partial payment for what the church has done to help you raise your family . . . keep your own priorities sorted out . . . tune you in to his ever-nearness.

Or perhaps, best yet, it's for you. For though the gift is to God, the benefit is for you. It's a moment for you to clip yet another strand from the rope of earth so that when he returns you won't be tied up.

PART 1:
FOLLOW-ALONG NOTES

USE THIS WORKSHEET AS YOU LISTEN TO "BECOMING MONEY SMART, PART 4."

· Each one should give as you have decided in your heart to give ... God loves the person who gives happily.

 2 Corinthians 9:7

· What happens in your heart when the offering occurs reflects

 _____.

· The purpose of the offering is _____

 _____.

- In giving, you proclaim to God:

1. This is how much I _____ you.   Mal. 1:6-14

   God is watching the _____.

   The process itself is an act of _____.

2. This is how much I _____ you.   Mal. 3:10-11

PART 2:
GOING DEEPER

PERSONAL STUDY AND REFLECTION

· Read David's prayer of thanksgiving in I Chronicles 29:10-20. What was
David's attitude towards giving to God?

_____

_____

_____

_____

_____

_____

- *When the offering occurs are you leaving the holy ground, or are you standing on higher ground?*

- Share obstacles you face in giving a tithe to God. What can be done to remove those obstacles?

_____

_____

_____

_____

_____

_____

_____

- In Philippians 4:17-19, Paul shares with fellow believers the good that comes from giving. Share in your own words the good that comes from giving to the Lord's work.

_____

_____

_____

_____

_____

_____

_____

_____

_____

- List ways offerings to the Lord can be used in the church.

_____

_____

_____

_____

_____

_____

_____

_____

_____

- Do you see the process of giving as an act of worship? When does that process begin for you?

_____

_____

_____

_____

_____

_____

_____

_____

_____ ■

PROMISES FROM
BECOMING MONEY SMART

Savor the following promises that God gives to those who determine to become money smart. One way that you can carry the message of this study with you everywhere in your heart is through the lost art of Scripture memorization. Select a few of the verses below to commit to memory.

Money that comes easily disappears quickly,
but money that is gathered little by little will grow.

PROVERBS 13:11

Whoever loves money will never have enough money;
whoever loves wealth will not be satisfied with it.

ECCLESIASTES 5:10

No one can serve two masters.
The person will hate one master and love the other,
or will follow one master and refuse to follow the other.
You cannot serve both God and worldly riches.

MATTHEW 6:24

It is better to be poor and respect the LORD
than to be wealthy and have much trouble.

PROVERBS 15:16

Those who work hard sleep in peace;
it is not important if they eat little or much.
But rich people worry about their wealth and cannot sleep.

ECCLESIASTES 5:12

Keep your lives free from the love of money,
and be satisfied with what you have.
God has said, "I will never leave you; I will never forget you."

HEBREWS 13:5

The love of money causes all kinds of evil.
Some people have left the faith, because they wanted to get more money,
but they have caused themselves much sorrow.

1 TIMOTHY 6:10

It is better to see what you have than to want more.
Wanting more is useless—like chasing the wind.

ECCLESIASTES 6:9

SUGGESTIONS FOR MEMBERS OF A GROUP STUDY

The Bible says that we should not forsake the assembling of ourselves together (see Hebrews 10:25). A small-group Bible study is one of the best ways to grow in your faith. As you meet together with other people, you will discover new truths about God's Word and challenge one another to greater levels of faith. The following are suggestions for you to get the most out of a small-group study of this material.

1. Come to the study prepared. Follow the suggestions for individual study mentioned previously. You will find that careful preparation will greatly enrich your time spent in group discussion.

2. Be willing to participate in the discussion. The leader of your group will not be lecturing. Instead, he or she will be encouraging the members of the group to discuss what they have learned. The leader will be asking the questions that are found in this guide.

3. Stick to the topic being discussed.

4. Be sensitive to the other members of the group. Listen attentively when they describe what they have learned. You may be surprised by their insights! Many questions do not have "right" answers, particularly questions that aim at meaning or application. Instead the questions push us to explore the passage more thoroughly.

5. When possible, link what you say to the comments of others. Also be affirming whenever you can. This will encourage some of the more hesitant members of the group to participate.

6. Expect God to teach you through the passage being discussed and through the other members of the group. Pray that you will have an enjoyable and profitable time together, but also that as a result of this study, you will find ways that you can take action individually and/or as a group.

7. Remember that anything said in the group is considered confidential and should not be discussed outside the group unless specific permission is given to do so.

LEADER'S GUIDE

1. Begin the session with prayer. Ask God to be with you as you begin to study his Word together.

2. Play the audio segment of the CD entitled "Becoming Money Smart, Part 1." Encourage group members to take notes in the section of their study guide entitled "Follow-Along Notes."

3. Begin group discussion by asking the following questions. Allow each group member ample time to answer, if they desire to do so.

   • Mismanaged money leads to stress. How does this relate to your life?

   • God gives many lessons on money in the Bible. Share one that has taught you a specific lesson.

   • How does God want you to view the possessions in your world?

   • Peter gave Jesus the boat to use in ministry. What possession do you allow Jesus to use in ministry?

- What example do you wish to leave to your children in money management?

4. Remind everyone to complete the "Going Deeper: Personal Study and Reflection" section for lesson two before the next group session.

5. Be sure to close in prayer. Invite the group participants to share prayer requests with the group and encourage them to pray for one another.

LESSON TWO: ATTITUDES TO AVOID

1. Begin the session with prayer. Ask God to be with you as you begin to study his Word together.

2. Play the audio segment of the CD entitled "Becoming Money Smart, Part 2." Encourage group members to take notes in the section of their study guide entitled "Follow-Along Notes."

3. Begin group discussion by asking the following questions. Allow each group member ample time to answer, if they desire to do so.

- Discuss what you consider the most dangerous attitude towards money.

- Are you tempted to think God only cares about how we use money as compared to our attitude towards money? Which do you feel is more important to God?

- Share more than one Scripture reference where God warns of the danger of "the love of money."

- List some consequences of having the wrong attitude about money.

- Give some practical steps to avoid the dangerous attitudes towards money shared in this lesson.

4. Remind everyone to complete the "Going Deeper: Personal Study and Reflection" section for lesson three before the next group session.

5. Be sure to close in prayer. Invite the group participants to share prayer requests with the group and encourage them to pray for one another.

LESSON THREE: DEALING WITH DEBT

1. Begin the session with prayer. Ask God to be with you as you begin to study his Word together.

2. Play the audio segment of the CD entitled "Becoming Money Smart, Part 3." Encourage group members to take notes in the section of their study guide entitled "Follow-Along Notes."

3. Begin group discussion by asking the following questions. Allow each group member ample time to answer, if they desire to do so.

   • How has debt taken its toll on society today?

   • Share ways debt hinders relationships.

   • Which question presented in the lesson do you often fail to ask yourself when faced with the choice to go into debt?

   • What damage is done to our testimony if we don't pay our debts?

   • Share some practical tools you have used to get control of debt.

4. Remind everyone to complete the "Going Deeper: Personal Study and Reflection" section for lesson four before the next group session.

5. Be sure to close in prayer. Invite the group participants to share prayer requests with the group and encourage them to pray for one another.

LESSON FOUR: THE GIFT OF GIVING

1. Begin the session with prayer. Ask God to be with you as you begin to study his Word together.

2. Play the audio segment of the CD entitled "Becoming Money Smart, Part 4." Encourage group members to take notes in the section of their study guide entitled "Follow-Along Notes."

3. Begin group discussion by asking the following questions. Allow each group member ample time to answer, if they desire to do so.

   • Is the act of giving to God a time that is honored or dreaded by most folks?

   • Is the time of offering treated as an act of worship in your church?

   • Share some blessings that come to a believer for being faithful to give to God.

   • Describe the difference between the tithe and the offering.

   • How is the command to give back to God for our own good?

4. Be sure to close in prayer. Invite the group participants to share prayer requests with the group and encourage them to pray for one another.

MAX LUCADO'S

MAX on life

S E R I E S

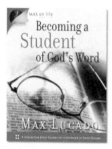

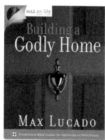

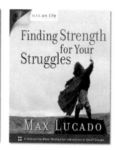

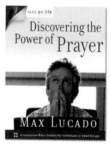

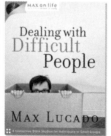

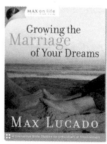

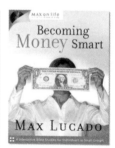

AVAILABLE WHEREVER BOOKS ARE SOLD.